MW00800887

HANDBOOK FOR READING & PREPARING
PROXY
STATEMENTS

A GUIDE TO THE SEC DISCLOSURE RULES FOR EXECUTIVE AND DIRECTOR COMPENSATION

SIXTH EDITION

Thomas M. Haines

WorldatWork.
Total Rewards Association

About WorldatWork®
The Total Rewards Association

WorldatWork is the leading nonprofit professional association in compensation and total rewards. We serve those who design and deliver total rewards programs to cultivate engaged, effective workforces that power thriving organizations. We accomplish this through education and certification; idea exchange; knowledge creation; information sharing; research; advocacy; and affiliation and networking. Founded in the United States in 1955, today WorldatWork serves total rewards professionals throughout the world working in organizations of all sizes and structures.

Certified Compensation Professional® (CCP®), Certified Benefits Professional® (CBP®), Global Remuneration Professional (GRP®), Certified Sales Compensation Professional (CSCP)® and Certified Executive Compensation Professional (CECP)® are registered trademarks of WorldatWork.

Any laws, regulations or other legal requirements noted in this publication are, to the best of the publisher's knowledge, accurate and current as of this book's publishing date. WorldatWork is providing this information with the understanding that WorldatWork is not engaged, directly or by implication, in rendering legal, accounting or other related professional services. You are urged to consult with an attorney, accountant or other qualified professional concerning your own specific situation and any questions that you may have related to that.

This book is published by WorldatWork Press. The interpretations, conclusions and recommendations in this book are those of the author and do not necessarily represent those of WorldatWork.

No portion of this publication may be reproduced in any form without express written permission from WorldatWork.

©2021 WorldatWork Press
Soft-cover ISBN: 978-1-57963-393-6
E-book ISBN: 978-1-57963-394-3
Editor: Brittany Smith
Graphic Design: Kris Sotelo

worldatwork.org

TABLE OF CONTENTS

INTRODUCTION

In 2006, the U.S. Securities and Exchange Commission (SEC) proposed and adopted extensive amendments to the proxy disclosure rules for executive and director compensation. Prior disclosure rules were criticized as being too rigid in terms of form and inadequate in terms of inclusiveness. Intended to provide investors with a clearer and more complete picture of executive and director compensation, the amended disclosure rules combine a revised and broader-based tabular presentation with an improved narrative disclosure that supplements the tables.

The disclosure rules have been updated over the years through SEC staff interpretive guidance, and have been significantly amended in 2009, 2010 and 2015. The 2009 amendments changed the reporting of stock and option awards from annual accounting accruals to grant date fair value, and added new disclosure requirements in regard to compensation consultant fees and compensation policies and practices as they relate to risk management. The 2010 amendments were in response to the sweeping Dodd-Frank financial reform legislation, and added new disclosures regarding shareholder advisory votes on executive compensation, compensation consultant independence, and golden parachute compensation. The 2015 amendments also were in response to Dodd-Frank legislation and added new disclosures regarding the ratio of total annual compensation for the principle executive officer to that of the median employee. In addition, new disclosures were proposed regarding hedging of company securities, pay versus performance and incentive compensation recovery or clawback policies. The hedging disclosure rules were finalized in 2018.

The disclosure rules begin with the requirement that shareholders be allowed a non-binding "say-on-pay" vote at least every three calendar years, a "say-when-on pay" vote at least every six calendar years, and a "say-on-parachute-pay" vote when shareholders are asked to approve a merger or similar transaction.

The rules continue with a narrative providing a general overview of the executive compensation program, referred to as the Compensation Discussion and Analysis (CD&A). As the name implies, this disclosure requires a discussion and analysis of the material factors underlying the executive compensation policies and decisions that are reflected in the amounts reported in the tables that follow. In a separate corporate governance section of the proxy statement, the rules require a scaled down version of the compensation committee report, as well as other compensation committee governance disclosures, including:

❙ The committee charter

❙ The processes and procedures for the consideration and determination of executive and director compensation

❙ The use of executive officers and compensation consultants in the compensation determination process

❙ Compensation consultant independence

❙ Disclosure of compensation consultant fees under certain circumstances

❙ Committee interlocks with company executives

❙ Disclosure of hedging company stock by employees, officers, and directors.

The stock performance graph that existed under prior disclosure rules is retained under the amended rules, but is moved to a separate section of the company's Form 10-K and is no longer considered part of executive compensation disclosure. Following the CD&A, the rules require a detailed disclosure of executive compensation that is organized in three broad categories.

The first category is a presentation of total compensation for the last three completed fiscal years, as reflected in the Summary Compensation Table. The Summary Compensation Table is supplemented for the last completed fiscal year by a Grants of Plan-Based Awards Table, which provides backup information for equity and incentive plan awards.

The second category is a presentation of holdings of equity-related interests, as reflected in an Outstanding Equity Awards at Fiscal Year-End Table. This table is intended to shed light on potential sources of future gains from previous equity awards. An Options Exercised and Shares Vested Table that summarizes realization of these equity award gains during the last completed fiscal year also is required.

The third category is a presentation of retirement and other post-employment compensation, as reflected in a Pension Benefits Table and a Nonqualified Deferred Compensation Table, along with a narrative summarizing potential payments upon employment termination or change in control.

In addition to these three categories, the rules require the following additional disclosures:

I Director Compensation Table and accompanying narrative disclosure that is similar to the Summary Compensation Table for executives, except that it covers only the last completed fiscal year

I Separate narrative disclosure of compensation programs for employees generally (not just executives) if the company determines that the risks associated with these programs are reasonably likely to have a material adverse effect on the company

I Comprehensive tabular and narrative disclosure of golden parachute compensation in the event shareholders are asked to approve a merger or similar transaction

I CEO pay ratio disclosure

I Proposed pay versus performance disclosure

I Proposed incentive compensation recovery policy and disclosure.

This book is directed at publicly held domestic companies that are not considered to be smaller reporting companies (SRC) or emerging growth companies (EGC), as defined by the SEC. Smaller reporting companies are defined generally as companies that have a common equity public float of less than $250 million or revenue of less than $100 million and public float of less than $700 million. Smaller reporting companies are subject to separate executive and director compensation rules that are intended to be less extensive and burdensome than the rules discussed here. For example, smaller reporting companies are required to provide abbreviated Summary Compensation Table disclosure for the CEO and two additional executive officers for the last two completed fiscal years, as well as the Outstanding Equity Awards at Fiscal Year-End and Director Compensation tables, but not other disclosures such as the CD&A or Grants of Plan-Based Awards Table. Emerging growth companies are defined generally as companies that have undergone an initial public offering (IPO) and have gross annual revenues of less than $1 billion. Emerging growth companies are subject to the same scaled disclosures applicable to smaller reporting companies discussed above for up to 5 years, and are exempt from the say-on-pay, say-when-on-pay, say-on-parachute pay, pay versus performance, and CEO pay ratio requirements for so long as an emerging growth company.

The compensation disclosure framework under the disclosure rules is illustrated in Figure I-1.

FIGURE I-1   Executive and Director Compensation Disclosure Framework

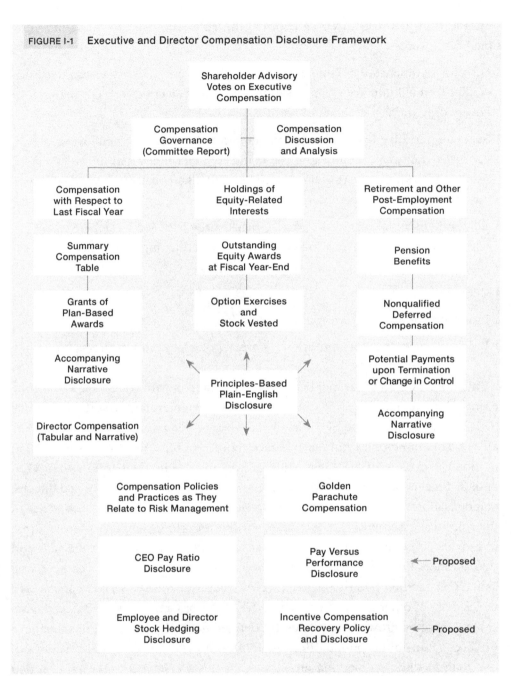

PRINCIPLES-BASED PLAIN ENGLISH DISCLOSURE

The disclosure rules are principles-based, meaning that they set forth broad disclosure concepts and provide various examples to illustrate those concepts. In addition, the rules require companies to apply plain-English principles when preparing executive and director compensation disclosures, as summarized in "What Companies Should Do" and "What Companies Should Avoid."

Additional tables are encouraged wherever tabular presentation facilitates clearer and more concise disclosure, such as a supplemental table for the All Other Compensation Column (i) of the Summary Compensation Table, or a breakdown of directors' fees for the Director Compensation Table.

What Companies Should Do

- Present information in clear and concise sections, paragraphs and sentences.
- Use short sentences and active voice.
- Use definite, concrete, everyday words.
- Use descriptive headings and subheadings.
- Use tables or bullet lists for complex material wherever possible.
- Use tables, schedules, charts and graphic illustrations that present relevant data in an understandable manner; graphs and charts must be drawn to scale and consistent with applicable disclosure requirements.

What Companies Should Avoid

- Use of legalistic or overly complex presentations that make the substance of the disclosure difficult to understand.
- Use of vague "boilerplate" explanations that are imprecise and readily subject to interpretation.
- Use of complex information copied directly from legal documents without clear and concise explanation of the provisions.
- Use of redundant information throughout the document, unless doing so enhances the quality of the information.
- Use of misleading tables or design elements.
- Use of multiple negatives.
- Use of legal jargon and highly technical terminology, business or otherwise.
- Use of frequent reliance on glossaries or defined terms as the primary means of explaining information.

[2]

NAMED EXECUTIVE OFFICERS

An important principle underlying the disclosures applicable to executive compensation is that the disclosures are required only for "named executive officers," who are identified as:

I **CEO and CFO (no matter how many officers):** All individuals serving as the principal executive officer (PEO) and principal financial officer (PFO) — or acting in a similar capacity — during the last completed fiscal year, regardless of total compensation level and whether they were serving as PEO or PFO on the last day of the last completed fiscal year.

I **Three most highly compensated officers:** The three most highly compensated "executive officers" serving at the end of the last completed fiscal year who did not serve as PEO or PFO at any time during that year, provided total compensation exceeds $100,000.

I **Up to two additional officers:** Up to two additional former executive officers who would have been included in the three most highly compensated category (based on the former executives' compensation for the full fiscal year), except that they were not serving as executive officers at the end of the last completed fiscal year.

An executive officer is defined generally as the president, any vice president in charge of a principal business unit, division or function (e.g., sales, administration, finance), and any other officer or person who performs significant policy-making functions (including officers of subsidiary companies). The definition of executive officer generally parallels the definition of "officer" for Section 16 reporting and short-swing profit requirements, except the Section 16 officer definition also explicitly includes the principal financial officer and the principal accounting officer or controller. In practice, however, many companies find that their lists of Section 16 officers and executive officers are identical.

Compensation rank is determined by reference to total compensation for the last completed fiscal year and calculated by subtracting the pension and above market interest amounts reported in Column (h) from the amount reported in Total Column (j) of the Summary Compensation Table.

It may be appropriate to include one or more executive officers of a subsidiary or other employees who perform significant policymaking functions as a named executive officer. In limited circumstances, it may be appropriate to exclude individuals (other than the PEO or PFO) who rank among the most highly compensated due to payments relating to overseas assignments. However, other payments that are not recurring and are unlikely to continue should be taken into consideration when determining named executive officer status. In addition, the following additional guidance is provided:

▌ The grant of a stock or option award that is subsequently forfeited in the same fiscal year should be taken into consideration when determining named executive officer status.

▌ If a company modifies an outstanding stock or option award to accelerate the vesting of an award that would otherwise be forfeited absent the acceleration, the entire fair value of the modified award should be taken into consideration in the year of modification when determining named executive officer status.

▌ If a company grants an equity incentive plan award that provides for negative discretion to comply with federal tax rules and results in a delayed grant date for accounting purposes, the award should be taken into consideration in the year awarded when determining named executive officer status.

▌ The grant of an annual nonequity incentive plan award that is subsequently declined by a named executive officer should be taken into consideration when determining named executive officer status.

▌ The decision by a named executive officer to not accept a discretionary bonus award before it is granted should not be taken into consideration when determining named executive officer status.

▌ Bonus amounts that are recovered by the company pursuant to a recoupment or clawback policy in a year subsequent to the year in which the bonus is earned should not be taken into consideration when determining named executive officer status for the year in which the bonus is recovered.

▌ Death benefits received from a company-funded life insurance policy should not be taken into consideration when determining named executive officer status.

Compensation information should be reported for the full fiscal year for any PEO, PFO or any other named executive officer who served as an executive officer for any part of a fiscal year. Compensation information for fiscal years prior to becoming a named executive officer does not need to be disclosed. If an individual is a named executive officer for the last completed fiscal year and the third preceding fiscal year, but not the second preceding fiscal year, compensation information must be disclosed in the Summary Compensation Table for all three fiscal years.

After a merger among operating companies there is no concept of "successor" compensation. Therefore, the surviving company in the merger need not report compensation paid by predecessor companies that disappeared in the merger, and compensation paid by predecessor companies need not be counted in determining whether an individual is a named executive officer of the surviving company. Equity compensation that is equitably assumed from the acquired company in an acquisition should not be taken into consideration when determining named executive officer status for acquired company executives who become acquirer company executives, and should not be reported in the Summary Compensation Table or Grants of Plan-Based Awards Table of the acquirer company. However, such equity compensation should be reported in the Outstanding Equity Awards at Fiscal Year-End Table and Options Exercised and Stock Vested Table of the acquirer company. Different rules may apply in situations involving a combination of companies (an amalgamation), an operating company combination with a "shell" company or a spinoff.

[3]

SHAREHOLDER ADVISORY VOTES ON EXECUTIVE COMPENSATION

Say-on-Pay Vote

At least once every three calendar years, in connection with a shareholder meeting at which directors are to be elected and executive compensation disclosures are required, companies must include a separate nonbinding shareholder advisory vote to approve the compensation of its named executive officers as disclosed in the CD&A and supporting tabular and narrative disclosures. This vote is referred to as a "say-on-pay" vote. An example of a resolution satisfying the requirements of a say-on-pay vote is set forth below:

> RESOLVED, that the compensation paid to the company's named executive officers, as disclosed pursuant to the compensation disclosure rules of the Securities and Exchange Commission, including the compensation discussion and analysis, the compensation tables and any related material disclosed in this proxy statement, is hereby APPROVED.

The say-on-pay vote does not apply to the director compensation disclosures discussed in Chapter 14 or the risk management disclosures applicable to non named executive officers discussed in Chapter 15, but does apply to any volitional golden parachute compensation disclosures discussed in Chapter 16 and the proposed pay versus performance disclosures discussed in Chapter 18. Companies are to briefly explain the nonbinding nature of the say-on-pay and say-when-on-pay votes (discussed below), and disclose the current frequency of say-on-pay votes and when the next vote will occur.

Say-When-on-Pay Vote

At least once every six calendar years, in connection with a shareholder meeting at which directors are to be elected and executive compensation disclosures are required, companies must include a separate nonbinding shareholder advisory vote as to whether the say-on-pay vote should occur every one, two or three years, or provide the choice to abstain from voting. This vote is referred to as a "say-when-on-pay" vote.

Companies must disclose their decisions as to the frequency of future say-on-pay votes based on the results of the most recent say-when-on-pay vote. This disclosure is made in the form of an amendment to the original Form 8-K disclosing the say when-on-pay vote results within 150 calendar days after the shareholder meeting, but no later than 60 calendar days prior to the next shareholder proposal submission deadline. Companies may include a recommendation as to how shareholders should vote, but the proxy must allow shareholders to vote for one of the four choices.

Companies may vote uninstructed proxies in accordance with management's recommendation for the say-when-on-pay vote only if the company includes a frequency recommendation, permits abstentions, and includes bold language regarding how uninstructed shares will be voted. Companies may exclude shareholder proposals relating to say-on-pay and say-when-on-pay votes on the grounds that they have been substantially implemented if the company adopts the frequency of say-on-pay alternative that received the majority support of votes cast (excluding abstentions) in the most recent say-when-on-pay vote.

Say-on-Parachute-Pay Vote

In connection with a shareholder meeting at which shareholders are asked to approve an acquisition, merger, consolidation, or proposed sale or disposition of all assets, companies must include a separate nonbinding shareholder advisory vote to approve any compensation arrangements related to the transaction that are reported pursuant to the golden parachute compensation disclosures discussed in Chapter 16. This vote is referred to as a "say-on-parachute-pay" vote. The say-on-parachute-pay vote does not apply to any arrangements between an acquiring company and the named executive officers of the target company, although such arrangements remain subject to the golden parachute compensation disclosures discussed in Chapter 16.

Absent one of the change in control transactions mentioned above, companies may voluntarily choose to incorporate the say-on-parachute-pay vote into their say-on-pay vote by including the golden parachute compensation disclosures discussed in Chapter 16 in addition to the non-change in control potential payments upon termination of employment disclosures discussed in Chapter 13. Companies making such volitional golden parachute compensation disclosures are relieved from the say-on-parachute-pay vote in subsequent change in control transactions (regardless of whether the say-on pay vote received majority support), unless the company adopts new arrangements or modifies existing golden parachute arrangements since the last say-on-pay vote. Such new or modified arrangements would be subject to the say-on-parachute-pay vote at the time of the transaction, and all arrangements would be subject to the golden parachute compensation disclosures discussed in Chapter 16.

New or modified arrangements are defined broadly to include the addition of new named executive officers, increases to compensation that would affect severance payments, and the grant of new equity awards since the last say-on-pay vote, regardless of materiality. Conversely, new or modified arrangements would not include decreases in compensation or changes in payments due to company stock price changes since the last say-on-pay vote (unless the stock price change triggers a tax gross up that was not previously disclosed).

Figure 2 provides an illustration of the golden parachute compensation that potentially would be subject to disclosure and vote under the rules, assuming the target company is the soliciting person.

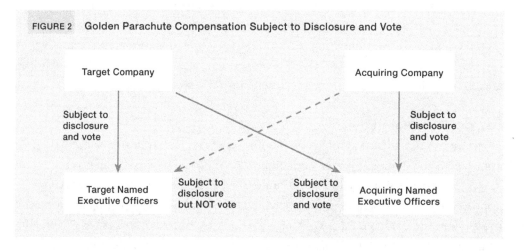

FIGURE 2   Golden Parachute Compensation Subject to Disclosure and Vote

Other Advisory Vote Provisions

Companies are not required to file preliminary proxy statements with the SEC in connection with say-on-pay or say-when-on-pay votes. Companies that are required to conduct an annual shareholder vote to approve executive compensation under the Troubled Asset Relief Program (TARP) are not required to comply with the say-on pay or say-when-on-pay votes until the first shareholder meeting that occurs after repayment of all outstanding TARP indebtedness. Companies that are foreign private issuers are not required to comply with the say-on-pay or say-when-on-pay votes, and are also not required to comply with the say-on-parachute-pay vote unless the target company is a domestic issuer (even if the acquirer is a foreign private issuer). Companies that are newly public are required to comply with the say-on-pay and say-when-on-pay votes beginning with the first shareholder meeting that occurs after the initial public offering. Last, broker discretionary voting of uninstructed shares is not permitted for any of the shareholder advisory votes discussed in this chapter.

[4   ]

COMPENSATION COMMITTEE GOVERNANCE

The rules consolidate disclosure requirements regarding director independence and related corporate governance disclosures in a separate section of the proxy statement. The rules that apply specifically to the compensation committee focus on the company's corporate governance structure that is in place for considering and determining executive and director compensation.

In contrast to these compensation committee governance disclosures, the CD&A discussed in Chapter 5 focuses on material information about the compensation policies and objectives of the company, and seeks to put the quantitative tabular disclosure about named executive officer compensation into perspective.

Compensation Committee Charter

State whether the compensation committee has a charter. If so, make a current copy available through the company's website or as an appendix to the proxy statement at least once every three years. If the company does not have a compensation committee, state the basis for not having one, and identify each director who participates in executive and director compensation decisions.

Compensation Committee Processes and Procedures

Provide a narrative description of the company's processes and procedures for the consideration and determination of executive and outside director compensation, including:

▌ Compensation committee's scope of authority

▌ Extent to which the compensation committee may delegate authority, specifying what authority and to whom

▌ Any role of executive officers in determining or recommending the amount or form of executive and director compensation

▌ Any role of compensation consultants in determining or recommending the amount or form of executive and director compensation, not just those who consulted with the compensation committee, other than any role limited solely to broad-based nondiscriminatory plans or the provision of non-customized survey information without related advice or recommendations.

Compensation Consultant Oversight

If compensation consultants have any role in determining or recommending the amount or form of executive and director compensation, provide the following additional information:

▌ Identify the consultant(s)

▌ State whether the consultant(s) is engaged directly by compensation committee or by another person

▌ Describe the nature and scope of assignment

▌ Describe the material elements of instructions or directions given to consultant(s) with respect to performance of engagement duties

▌ Discuss whether work of the consultant has raised any conflict of interest and, if so, the nature of the conflict and how the conflict is being addressed (not applicable to legal counsel or other advisers).

Compensation Consultant Independence

Compensation committees must have sole discretion and adequate funding to retain or obtain the services of (and be directly responsible for the appointment, compensation, and oversight of) a compensation consultant, independent legal counsel, or other adviser, and such advisers may be retained only after consideration of the following six specified independence-related factors:

▌ The provision of other nonexecutive/director compensation consulting services to the company by the consulting firm

▌ The amount of company fees received by the consulting firm as a percentage of the consulting firm's total revenue

▌ The policies and procedures of the consulting firm designed to prevent conflicts of interest

▌ Any business or personal relationship between the individual consultant and compensation committee members

▌ Any stock of the company owned by the individual consultant

▌ Any business or personal relationship between the consulting firm or the individual consultant and an executive officer of the company.

In addition, the rules require compensation committees to consider any other factors that would be relevant to the adviser's independence from management. Importantly, the rules require only that compensation committee conduct an independence assessment taking into consideration the factors listed above, the rules do not require compensation committees to retain independent advisers. In addition, companies need not consider the factors listed above when engaging the services of in-house legal counsel.

Compensation Consultant Fees

In addition, disclosure of fees related to the retention of compensation consultants is required under the following circumstances:

▌ If the compensation committee or board engages its own consultant and that consultant provides other nonexecutive/director compensation consulting services to the company in excess of $120,000 during the last completed fiscal year

▌ If the compensation committee or board does not engage its own consultant and another consultant provides both executive/director compensation consulting services and other nonexecutive/director compensation consulting services in excess of $120,000 during the last completed fiscal year.

If either of the aforementioned situations exist, companies must disclose the aggregate fees paid for both executive/director and nonexecutive/director compensation consulting services. In cases in which the compensation consultant is retained by the compensation committee, companies must further disclose whether management recommended the nonexecutive/director compensation consulting services and whether the compensation committee or board approved such services. However, companies are not required to disclose the nature and extent of the nonexecutive/director compensation consulting services. Fee disclosure for consultants that work with management is not required if the compensation committee or board has its own consultant, regardless of the amount or type of services provided.

Fee disclosure is not required for consultants that perform services involving only broad-based nondiscriminatory plans or the provision of non-customized survey information without related advice or recommendations, provided these are the only services provided by the consultant. If the consultant's role extends beyond these services and the $120,000 disclosure threshold for nonexecutive/director compensation consulting services is triggered, all services must be disclosed.

For purposes of this disclosure, there is no limitation on the types of services that are included in the definition of nonexecutive/director compensation consulting services, and such services can include services to executives as well as nonexecutives and revenue from the sale of products to the company. If disclosure is required, the classification of broad-based nondiscriminatory or non-customized survey services as executive/director or nonexecutive/director compensation consulting services depends on whether the executives/directors benefit from such services under the facts and circumstances. That is, if executives/directors benefit from the services, they should be classified as executive/director compensation consulting fees, and vice versa. Other services such as benefits administration, human resources services, actuarial services, merger integration services, and non-customized survey information for nonexecutive/director compensation should be classified as nonexecutive/director compensation consulting services.

Compensation Committee Interlocks

Under the caption "Compensation Committee Interlocks and Insider Participation," identify each person who served as a member of the compensation committee during the last completed fiscal year, indicating each member who:

▌ Is a current officer or employee of the company

▌ Has any relationship requiring related party disclosure pursuant to Item 404 of Regulation S-K

▌ Has an interlocking compensation committee/board relationship with an executive officer of the company, as shown in Figure 3.

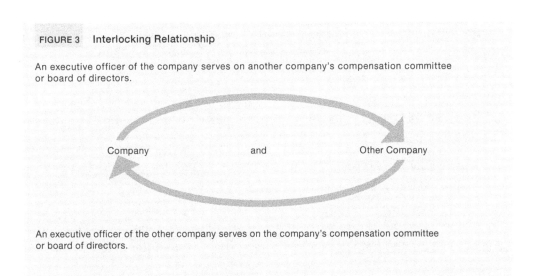

FIGURE 3   Interlocking Relationship

An executive officer of the company serves on another company's compensation committee or board of directors.

Company   and   Other Company

An executive officer of the other company serves on the company's compensation committee or board of directors.

Compensation Committee Report

Under the caption "Compensation Committee Report," state whether the compensation committee has reviewed and discussed the CD&A with management. Based on that review and discussion, state whether the compensation committee has recommended to the board of directors the inclusion of the CD&A in the proxy statement or annual report. The names of each member of the compensation committee must appear below the Compensation Committee Report.

The Compensation Committee Report is not deemed to be soliciting material, nor is it to be filed with the SEC. The PEO and PFO can look to the Compensation Committee Report in providing their required certifications under the Sarbanes-Oxley Act of 2002.

Employee, Officer and Director Hedging

In proxy statements with respect to the election of directors, companies (including emerging growth companies and smaller reporting companies, but excluding foreign private issuers) are required to disclose any practices or policies related to the ability of employees (including officers) and directors to purchase financial instruments or otherwise engage in transactions that are designed to hedge or offset any decrease in the company's stock price:

▎ Disclosure is required either of the policies in full or a summary of the policies

▎ Such hedging transactions include prepaid variable forward contracts, equity swaps, collars, and exchange funds

▎ Company stock includes any equity securities granted by the company as compensation or held directly or indirectly by the employees and directors

▎ Equity securities include shares issued by the company and its parents, subsidiaries or subsidiaries of the company's parents that are registered on a national exchange or with the SEC

▎ Disclosure is required for permitted and prohibited categories of hedging transactions, as well as whether such categories vary among employee and director populations.

▎ If the company has no practices or policies, it should disclose that fact or that hedging is generally permitted

In addition, companies are permitted to cross-reference their discussion of risk hedging policies applicable to named executive officers in the CD&A (if any) to these required disclosures provided they satisfy the CD&A requirements.

[5]

COMPENSATION DISCUSSION AND ANALYSIS

The purpose of the CD&A is to provide material information that is necessary to gain an understanding of the compensation policies and decisions regarding the named executive officers. The discussion should focus on the material principles underlying executive compensation policies and decisions, as well as the most important factors relevant to analysis of those policies and decisions. However, the discussion should not resort to boilerplate language and repetition of more detailed information set forth in the tables, footnotes and narrative disclosures that follow. Notwithstanding this instruction, many CD&As have become lengthy and dense over time. In response to investor feedback, a best practice has emerged whereby companies insert an "executive summary" section at the beginning of the CD&A.

The discussion and analysis must address the following with respect to the executive compensation program:

▎ Program objectives

▎ What the program is designed to reward

▎ Each element of compensation

▎ Why each element was chosen

▎ How the amount of each element is determined

▎ How each element is linked to program objectives and other pay elements

▎ Whether and how the company has considered the results of the most recent say-on-pay vote.

Material factors discussed and analyzed will vary depending on the facts and circumstances, but the rules are principles-based and provide various examples of information that may be disclosed, including:

▎ Allocation between long- and short-term compensation

▌ Allocation between cash and noncash compensation, and different forms of noncash compensation

▌ Allocation among different types of long-term compensation, including cost/benefit analysis

▌ Determination of cash and equity award grant dates

▌ Use of corporate and individual performance measures

▌ Exercise of discretion, either to provide relief in event of failure to attain performance goals, or to increase/decrease payments

▌ Adjustment or recovery of previous payments in event of financial restatement, including the reasons for the clawback and how the amount recovered was determined

▌ Consideration of realized/unrealized prior compensation amounts in determination of retirement benefits

▌ Selection of award payment triggers in the event of employment termination or change in control

▌ Consideration of accounting and tax rules

▌ Stock ownership requirements/guidelines and risk-hedging policies (disclosure of risk-hedging policies may be incorporated by reference to the "employee, officer and director hedging" section of the proxy statement)

▌ Consideration of compensation benchmarking practices, which entails using compensation data about other companies as a reference point to provide a framework for compensation decisions

▌ Role of executive officers in determining compensation.

If the company has a program, plan or practice to time stock option or other equity award grants to executives in coordination with the release of material nonpublic information, the discussion and analysis should address the following questions:

▌ Are grants to executives timed in coordination with the release of material nonpublic information?

▌ Are grants to nonexecutives similarly timed? If not, why?

▌ What is the role of the compensation committee in approving and administering the timed grants?

▌ How does the compensation committee take such information into account when determining whether and in what amounts to make grants?

▌ Does the compensation committee delegate any aspect of the actual administration of the program to anyone else?

▌ What is the role of executive officers in the company's practice of option timing?

▌ Does the company set the grant date of options granted to new executives in coordination with the release of material nonpublic information?

▌ Does the company plan to time, or has it timed, its release of material nonpublic information for the purpose of affecting the value of executive compensation?

In addition, discussion of the determination of the stock option exercise price is required if the exercise price is:

▌ Based on the stock's price on a date other than the actual grant date, or

▌ Determined by using a formula based on average (or lowest) prices of the company's stock in a period preceding, surrounding or following the grant date.

Unlike the Compensation Committee Report discussed in Chapter 4, the CD&A is considered soliciting material that is filed with the SEC. As such, this information is subject to the certifications that PEOs and PFOs are required to make under the Sarbanes-Oxley Act, as well as the company's disclosure controls and procedures. The CD&A should focus on the information contained in the tables, footnotes and related narrative for the named executive officers for the last completed fiscal year. Compensation actions taken in previous years or after the last completed fiscal year (such as discussion of performance targets/goals for future fiscal years) should be included only if it enhances the understanding of the named executive officers' compensation for the last completed fiscal year.

When evaluating whether performance targets may be omitted from disclosure, companies first must determine if such disclosure is material to gain an under-standing of compensation paid for the last completed fiscal year. If it is not material, no disclosure is required. If it is material, quantitative performance targets must be disclosed unless the goals involve confidential trade secrets or commercial or financial information that would result in competitive harm to the company if disclosed. There is no requirement to disclose quantitative targets for inherently subjective or qualitative assessments, such as "demonstrated leadership."

In making a competitive harm assessment, companies are to apply the same stan-dards used when requesting confidential treatment of trade secrets or commercial or financial information from the SEC, without having to make an actual request.

However, if such performance goals are not disclosed, the company must discuss how difficult/likely it would be for the executive/company to achieve the undisclosed goals, and the company may be required to demonstrate to the SEC why the disclosure would result in competitive harm. To the extent that performance goals have otherwise been publicly disclosed, the nondisclosure exception is not permitted. Disclosure of non-GAAP performance goals (and actual company performance versus those goals) is not subject to the general rules regarding disclosure of non-GAAP financial measures, but the company still must disclose how the non-GAAP amounts are calculated from the amounts actually reported in the audited financial statements. This exception is limited solely to disclosure of performance goals, and does not apply to disclosure of non-GAAP financial measures presented elsewhere in the CD&A or proxy statement.

[6]

SUMMARY COMPENSATION TABLE

Summary Compensation Table
(for the last completed fiscal year ending xx/xx/20xx)

Name and Principal Position	Year	Salary ($)	Bonus ($)	Stock Awards ($)
(a)	(b)	(c)	(d)	(e)

The rules explicitly require the disclosure of all plan and nonplan compensation awarded to, earned by or paid to the named executive officers, unless specifically excluded by the rules. Examples of compensation that may be excluded from disclosure (except in regard to golden parachute compensation disclosure) are nondiscriminatory group life, disability, health, hospitalization and medical reimbursement plans available to all salaried employees. Benefits received under relocation plans may not be excluded from disclosure, and presumably should be treated as a perquisite even if nondiscriminatory. One or more columns may be omitted if no amounts are reportable for any fiscal year covered by the table. Also, it is permissible to add one or more columns as long as it does not make the disclosure misleading or unclear. If the rules do not specifically limit footnote disclosure to the last completed fiscal year, footnote disclosure for prior reported years is required only if material to an understanding of compensation for the last completed fiscal year.

Under proposed incentive compensation recovery policy and disclosure rules, any amounts of incentive compensation recovered pursuant to a company's incentive compensation recovery policy shall reduce the amount reported in the applicable column of the Summary Compensation Table for the fiscal year in which the amount recovered initially was reported, with appropriate footnote disclosure of such reduction.

Year (b)

Information is required for the last three completed fiscal years, or a shorter period if the company is not an SEC registrant for all three years (e.g., in an initial public offering prospectus). The rules permitted a phase-in during the first two years of reporting under the rules, such that only one year of information was required in the first year, and only two years of information were required in the second year.

Option Awards ($)	Nonequity Incentive Plan Compensation ($)	Change in Pension Value and Nonqualified Deferred Compensation Earnings ($)	All Other Compensation ($)	Total ($)
(f)	(g)	(h)	(i)	(j)

Salary (c) and Bonus (d)

Salary and bonus should be based on cash and noncash amounts that are earned for the applicable fiscal year, regardless of whether paid currently or deferred. These columns should include any amount of salary or bonus converted to some other form of noncash compensation at the election of a named executive officer. Footnote disclosures should describe such noncash compensation and refer to the Grants of Plan-Based Awards Table, if applicable.

If the amount of salary or bonus forgone is less than the value of the equity compensation received, the incremental value of the equity compensation should be reported in the Stock Awards Column (e) or Option Awards Column (f) of this table, as appropriate. Similarly, if the conversion election is embedded in the terms of the equity award such that the award falls within the scope of Financial Accounting Standards Board Accounting Standards Codification Topic 718 (FASB ASC Topic 718), the value of the equity compensation should be reported in Columns (e) or (f), as appropriate. If salary or bonus amounts are not calculable at the time of proxy issuance, companies are to provide footnote disclosure stating that fact, along with the date such amounts are expected to be determined. Form 8-K disclosure is required when the amount is determined, stating the amount and recalculating the Total Column (j).

Cash bonus awards should be reported in the Bonus Column (d) if they are:

❙ Discretionarily or subjectively determined; however, the decision by a named executive officer not to accept a discretionary bonus award before it is granted should not be reported in the Summary Compensation Table

❙ Not based on pre-established, substantially uncertain and communicated performance criteria

❙ Sign-on bonuses or amounts paid in excess of amounts earned by meeting the performance criteria in a nonequity incentive plan.

Cash retention bonuses that are conditioned on future service should not be reported in the Bonus Column (d) until the fiscal year in which they are earned. Cash bonus awards that are based on pre-established, substantially uncertain and communicated performance criteria should be reported in the Nonequity Incentive Plan Compensation Column (g), regardless of the duration of the performance period or whether negative discretion is permissible.

Bonus amounts that are recovered by the company pursuant to a recoupment or clawback policy in a year subsequent to the year in which the bonus is earned should be reported as an adjustment to the Bonus Column (d) and Total Column (j) for the year in which the bonus is earned, as opposed to the year the compensation is recovered, with appropriate footnote disclosure of the amount recovered.

Stock Awards (e) and Option Awards (f)

Column (e) applies to equity and liability awards that do not have option-like features, such as restricted stock, performance shares and share units. Column (f) applies to equity and liability awards with option-like features, such as stock options and stock appreciation rights (SARs).

For both columns, companies are to disclose the aggregate grant date fair value of stock and option awards granted during the last completed fiscal year computed in accordance with the equity compensation accounting provisions of FASB ASC Topic 718, excluding the effect of estimated forfeitures. Stock and option awards with a performance condition are computed based on the probable outcome of the performance condition(s) as of the grant date (that is, the target amount), with footnote disclosure of the maximum probable payment. This grant date probable outcome must be reported even if the actual outcome of the performance condition(s), and therefore the number of shares actually earned, is known by the time the proxy statement is filed. The dollar value of dividends or dividend equivalents paid on stock and option awards is not required to be disclosed, provided the dividends or dividend equivalents are properly factored into the grant date fair value. If stock options or SARs are repriced during the last completed fiscal year, companies are to report the incremental fair value of such repricing for that year. Companies are to include a footnote disclosing all assumptions in the stock and option award valuations by reference to the financial statements, footnotes to financial statements, or Management's Discussion and Analysis. Companies may also make reference to the Grants of Plan-Based Awards Table if these assumptions are disclosed in that table.

If an equity or liability award is granted after the end of the last completed fiscal year for which it was earned, disclosure of the award should be made in the CD&A for the last completed fiscal year, but the award should not be reported in this table or the Grants of Plan-Based Awards Table until the following fiscal year in which it is granted. Equity compensation that is equitably assumed from the acquired company in an acquisition should not be reported in the Summary Compensation Table or the Grants of Plan-Based Awards Table of the acquirer company. The grant of a stock or option award that is subsequently forfeited in the same fiscal year should be reported in the Summary Compensation Table and Grants of Plan-Based Awards Table. If a company modifies an outstanding stock or option award to accelerate the vesting of an award that would otherwise be forfeited absent the acceleration, the entire fair value of the modified award should be reported in the Summary Compensation Table and Grants of Plan-Based Awards Table, regardless of whether the modification occurs in the same or subsequent year of grant.

If a company grants an equity incentive plan award that provides for negative discretion to comply with federal tax rules and results in a delayed grant date for accounting purposes, the award should be reported in the Summary Compensation Table and Grants of Plan-Based Awards Table for the year in which the term of the award and performance targets are communicated to the named executive officer

and the service inception date begins, not the later grant date for accounting purposes. The amount reported in both tables should be the then-probable outcome of the performance condition(s) as of the service inception date.

Nonequity Incentive Plan Compensation (g)

This column represents cash amounts earned in connection with short- and long-term nonequity incentive plan awards that do not fall within the scope of FASB ASC Topic 718 (e.g., performance-based annual bonus and performance unit awards). In general, nonequity incentive plan awards are reported in this column only if they are in no way linked to the underlying value of the company's stock. That is, the awards are not denominated in company stock, the award vesting conditions are not based on the company's stock price, or the award payment or settlement provisions are not made in company stock. All earnings on nonequity incentive plan compensation (including amounts attributable to any outstanding awards) must be identified and quantified in a footnote, and are reportable even if not payable until a later year.

The grant of an annual nonequity incentive plan award that is subsequently declined by a named executive officer should be reported in the Summary Compensation Table and Grants of Plan-Based Awards Table, with appropriate disclosure of the compensation declined in the CD&A and Summary Compensation Table by either a footnote or an adjoining column to the nonequity incentive plan compensation column.

Change in Pension Value and Nonqualified Deferred Compensation Earnings (h)

Column (h) represents the sum of:

❙ The aggregate year-over-year increase in the actuarial present value of accumulated pension benefits under all tax-qualified and supplemental nonqualified defined benefit plans (but excluding tax-qualified and nonqualified defined contribution plans), and

❙ Above-market or preferential earnings on nonqualified deferred compensation and defined contribution plans.

Such amounts should be separately identified and quantified in footnotes, and any aggregate net negative change in pension value should be disclosed in footnotes but not reported in Column (h).

Increase in pension value is calculated as the difference between the amount reported in Column (d) of the Pension Benefits Table for the last completed fiscal year (increased by any plan payments made during the year) and the amount reported in the same column/table for the next preceding year. It includes increases in value due to additional years of service, compensation increases and plan amendments (if any), as well as increases (or decreases) in value attributable to interest. Companies with multiple pension plans are permitted to aggregate all increases or decreases in the actuarial present value of accumulated pension benefits before applying the "no negative number" provisions of this table.

Interest is above market if it is in excess of 120 percent of the applicable federal long-term rate at the date the rate is set or discretionarily reset, with compounding that corresponds most closely to that of the plan. Only the above-market portion of interest is reported, assuming satisfaction of all conditions necessary to receive the highest plan rate. Earnings on nonqualified deferred compensation are not above market or preferential if calculated in the same manner and rate as earnings on externally managed investments for employees participating in a broad-based tax-qualified plan. However, this provision may not be available for supplemental retirement plans that do not have any relationship to a tax-qualified retirement plan of the company.

Dividends and dividend equivalents on stock- denominated deferred compensation are preferential if they are in excess of amounts paid on the company's common stock. Only the preferential portions of dividends and dividend equivalents are reported.

All Other Compensation (i)

Column (i) represents amounts not properly reportable in any other column, including:

I The incremental cost of perquisites to the company, unless less than $10,000

I Tax gross-ups, regardless of amount

I Company contributions to qualified and nonqualified defined contribution plans

I Preferential stock purchase discounts other than discount stock purchase plans available to all salaried employees, such as Section 423 plans, or dividend reinvestment plans available to all shareholders

I Preferential life insurance premiums, but not death benefits received

I Dividends or other earnings paid or accrued that were not factored into the grant date fair value of stock or option awards

I Amounts paid or accrued in connection with termination of employment or change in control, including defined benefit payments that are accelerated upon change in control.

For the last completed fiscal year, any item other than perquisites in this column must be identified and quantified if in excess of $10,000. For amounts paid or accrued in connection with termination of employment or change in control, an amount is accrued and should be disclosed if all performance necessary to earn the amount is complete. Conversely, an amount is not accrued (and thus should not be disclosed) if future performance or compliance with a restrictive covenant is required for payment to become due. For example, if a named executive officer has completed all performance to earn an amount, but the payment is subject to deferral, the amount is considered earned and should be disclosed. Conversely, if an amount would be payable in the future subject to the named executive officer's cooperation or compliance with a noncompete, the amount is not reportable because future performance is required. Notwithstanding the above, future amounts payable that are not required to be reported in this column should be disclosed in the potential payments upon termination or change in control section discussed in Chapter 13.

Tabular presentation of this column is encouraged under plain-English principles if doing so enhances disclosure. See Chapter 7 for a further explanation of the perquisite disclosure rules and an example of tabular presentation of this column.

Total (j)

All amounts in this table must be reported as a single numerical value in U.S. dollars, with footnote disclosure of any necessary exchange-rate conversions.

This table must include all amounts earned, including director fees, regardless of whether paid currently or deferred.

Narrative Disclosure

The material factors that are necessary to understand the amounts disclosed in the Summary Compensation Table are required in an accompanying narrative disclosure. These factors include material terms of employment agreements, method of calculating earnings on deferred compensation, and an explanation of salary and bonus in proportion to total compensation.

[7]

ALL OTHER COMPENSATION

All Other Compensation
(not required; example of plain-English tabular presentation)

Name	Perquisites ($)	Tax Gross-Ups ($)	Defined Contribution Savings Plan Company Contributions ($)	Preferential Stock Purchase Discounts ($)
(a)	(b)	(c)	(d)	(e)

Perquisites (b)

An item is not a perquisite if it is integrally and directly related to the perfor-mance of the executive's or director's duties. That is, the executive or director needs the personal benefit to do the job. Examples of items not considered perquisites include a personal digital assistant (PDA) or laptop computer if the company believes it is an integral part of the executive's or director's duties to be accessible by email.

Conversely, an item is a perquisite if it confers a direct or indirect benefit that has a personal aspect, unless it is available on a nondiscriminatory basis to all employees. The fact that an expense may be an ordinary and necessary business expense for tax or other purposes, or that the expense is for the convenience of the company, is irrelevant. Examples of perquisites include:

▌ Club memberships not used exclusively for business entertainment purposes

▌ Personal financial or tax advice

▌ Personal travel or use of other property financed by the company

▌ Housing or other living expenses

▌ Relocation plans, even if nondiscriminatory

▌ Security provided at personal residence or during personal travel

▌ Commuting expenses

▌ Discriminatory discounts on company products or services.

For the last completed fiscal year, all perquisites must be identified by type if the aggregate amount is $10,000 or more. In addition, each perquisite in excess of $25,000 (or 10 percent of all perquisites, if greater) must be quantified, with footnote disclosure of the company's incremental cost valuation methodology.

Preferential Insurance Premiums ($)	Dividends Not Factored in Grant Date Fair Value of Equity Awards ($)	Payments in Regard to Termination of Employment ($)	Total ($)
(f)	(g)	(h)	(i)

If the $10,000 reporting threshold for perquisites is exceeded, each perquisite must be separately identified by type even if there is no incremental company cost, but reporting is not required for perquisites that are fully reimbursed by the executive.

Tax gross-up payments must be reported in the Summary Compensation Table for the same year as the related perquisites or other compensation is disclosed, and not in the year actually paid (if later).

[8]

GRANTS OF PLAN-BASED AWARDS

Grants of Plan-Based Awards
(for the last completed fiscal year ending xx/xx/20xx)

Name	Grant Date	Approval or Action Date, if Different	Nonequity Incentive Plan Awards: Number of Units or Other Rights (#)	Estimated Future/Possible Payouts Under Nonequity Incentive Plan Awards		
				Threshold ($)	Target ($)	Maximum ($)
(a)	(b)	(if applicable)	(if applicable)	(c)	(d)	(e)

Disclosure for each award reported in this table must be provided in a separate row. If awards are made under more than one plan, the plan under which the award is granted must be identified. Disclosure is required for "reload" stock options, as well as for stock and option awards of a parent or subsidiary company. Equity compensation that is equitably assumed from the acquired company in an acquisition should not be reported in the Grants of Plan-Based Awards Table of the acquirer company. This table (or one or more columns) may be omitted if no amounts are reportable for the last completed fiscal year covered by the table. Also, it is permissible to add one or more columns as long as it does not make the disclosure misleading or unclear.

Grant Date (b)

Column (b) represents the grant date for equity-based awards. If the grant date is different than the date action was taken by the compensation committee (or other administering committee or board of directors), a separate adjoining column showing that other date must be added between Columns (b) and (c).

Estimated Future Payouts Under Nonequity Incentive Plan Awards (c)-(e)

These columns represent estimated potential future cash payments of short- and long-term nonequity incentive plan awards that do not fall within the scope of FASB ASC Topic 718, such as performance-based annual bonus and performance unit awards. If nonequity incentive plan awards are denominated in units or other rights, a separate adjoining column must be added between Columns (b) and (c) to quantify the number of units or other rights awarded. For cash awards that are made in the same year they are earned under an annual nonequity incentive plan (and the amounts are disclosed in the Nonequity Incentive Plan Compensation Column (g) in the Summary Compensation Table), companies are permitted to change "Future" to "Possible" in the header for Columns (c) through (e) of this table.

Estimated Future Payouts Under Equity Incentive Plan Awards			All Other Stock Awards: Number of Shares of Stock or Units (#)	All Other Option Awards: Number of Securities Under-lying Options (#)	Exercise or Base Price of Option Awards ($)	Closing Price on Date of Grant for Option Awards, if Different ($)	Grant Date Fair Value of Stock and Option Awards ($)
Threshold (#) or ($)	Target (#) or ($)	Maximum (#) or ($)					
(f)	(g)	(h)	(i)	(j)	(k)	(if applicable)	(l)

Estimated Future Payouts Under Equity Incentive Plan Awards (f)-(h)

These columns represent the estimated potential future number of share/share unit payments of short- and long-term equity incentive plan awards that fall within the scope of FASB ASC Topic 718 (e.g., performance- or market-based stock options and performance shares). Disclosure also is required for repriced or materially modified option awards, except for repricings that occur in connection with a pre-existing formula, an antidilution provision or a recapitalization transaction. If an equity incentive plan award is denominated in dollars but payable in stock, it should be reported in Columns (f) through (h) of this table, with footnote disclosure explaining the stock payout provisions. Also, companies may change the (#) to ($) in the column titles if all awards in those columns are structured that way.

Estimated Future Target Payouts Under Nonequity and Equity Incentive Plan Awards (d) and (g)

If an incentive plan award provides only for a single estimated payout, companies are to report that amount as a target award in Columns (d) or (g), as appropriate. If an incentive plan award target is not determinable, companies are to report a representative amount based on the previous fiscal year's performance as a target award in Columns (d) or (g), as appropriate.

All Other Stock and Option Awards (i) and (j)

These columns represent the number of stock and option awards granted that are not subject to a performance or market condition, such as service-based restricted stock and stock options (i.e., nonincentive plan equity awards). Disclosure also is required for repriced or materially modified option awards, except for repricings that occur in connection with a pre-existing formula, an antidilution provision or a recapitalization transaction. If a nonincentive plan equity award is granted in tandem with an incentive plan award, companies are to report only the nonincentive Estimated Future Payouts Under Equity Incentive Plan Awards plan equity award in Columns (i) or (j), with accompanying footnote disclosure or textual narrative of the tandem feature, as appropriate.

Exercise or Base Price of Option Awards (k)

If the exercise price is less than the closing price of the company's stock on the grant date, a separate adjoining column must be added between Columns (k) and (l) showing the closing price. Also,   accompanying footnote disclosure or textual narrative is required to explain the methodology for determining the exercise or base price if different than the closing price. Footnote disclosure also is required if any consideration is paid by the named executive officer for the award.

Grant Date Fair Value of Stock and Option Awards (l)

Column (l) represents the grant date fair value of each equity award granted during the last completed fiscal year computed in accordance with FASB ASC Topic 718, including the incremental fair value of repriced or materially modified option or equity incentive plan awards (except for repricings that occur in connection with a pre-existing formula, an antidilution provision or a recapitalization transaction). The grant date fair value of stock and option awards with a performance condition is computed based on the probable outcome of the performance condition(s) as of the grant date (that is, the target amount), with footnote disclosure of the maximum probable payment.

Narrative Disclosure

The material factors that are necessary to understand the amounts disclosed in the Grants of Plan-Based Awards Table are required in an accompanying narrative disclosure. These factors include material equity award repricings or other material modifications during the last completed fiscal year (e.g., extensions to the exercise period or changes to the vesting schedule), vesting and earnout schedules, and dividend treatment.

[9]

OUTSTANDING EQUITY AWARDS AT FISCAL YEAR-END

Outstanding Equity Awards at Fiscal Year End
(for the last completed fiscal year ending xx/xx/20xx)

	Option Awards				
Name	Number of Securities Underlying Unexercised Options: Exercisable (#)	Number of Securities Underlying Unexercised Options: Unexercisable (#)	Equity Incentive Plan Awards: Number of Securities Underlying Unexercised Unearned Options (#)	Option Exercise Price ($)	Option Expiration Date
(a)	(b)	(c)	(d)	(e)	(f)

Outstanding unearned stock and option awards with time-vesting conditions (i.e., nonincentive plan equity awards) are reportable in Columns (b), (c), (g) and (h), as appropriate. Also included in these columns are unexercised option awards and nonvested stock awards that previously were reported as equity incentive plan awards but have been subsequently earned.

Outstanding unearned stock and option awards with performance-vesting conditions (i.e., equity incentive plan awards) are reportable in Columns (d), (i) and (j), as appropriate. Equity compensation that is equitably assumed from the acquired company in an acquisition should be reported in the Outstanding Equity Awards at Fiscal Year-End Table of the acquirer company. This table (or one or more columns) may be omitted if no amounts are reportable for the last completed fiscal year covered by the table. Also, it is permissible to add one or more columns as long as it does not make the disclosures misleading or unclear.

Option Awards (b)-(f)

Outstanding option awards must be reported on an award-by-award basis, including separate tranches of a single award with different exercise prices or expiration dates. However, the awards may be aggregated if the exercise price and expiration date are identical. This disclosure should include option awards that have been transferred without value, such as by gifts or other transfers in which the executive receives no consideration for the award.

Stock Awards (g)-(j)

Outstanding stock awards are aggregated and reported as a single row, with aggregate market value based on the closing market stock price at the end of the last completed fiscal year. Dividends or dividend equivalents paid on outstanding stock awards that are credited and reinvested into additional stock awards should

Stock Awards			
Number of Shares or Units of Stock that Have Not Vested (#)	Market Value of Shares or Units of Stock that Have Not Vested ($)	Equity Incentive Plan Awards: Number of Unearned Shares, Units or Other Rights that Have Not Vested (#)	Equity Incentive Plan Awards: Market or Payout Value of Unearned Shares, Units or Other Rights that Have Not Vested ($)
(g)	(h)	(i)	(j)

be reported in this table while unvested and, upon vesting, in the Option Exercises and Stock Vested Table. Shares acquired upon option exercise that are subject to a company repurchase obligation (at the exercise price) are reported in Columns (g) and (h) until the repurchase obligation lapses. Then, the shares are reported in Columns (d) and (e) of the Option Exercises and Stock Vested Table.

Equity incentive plan awards that are earned as of the last completed fiscal year end but paid in restricted stock should be reported in columns (g) and (h) rather than (i) and (j) of the Outstanding Awards at Fiscal Year-End Table, based on the actual number of equity incentive plan awards earned (even if the actual number of shares earned is determined after fiscal year end).

Vesting Dates and Transferability (b)-(j)

Footnote disclosure is required to identify the vesting dates for each outstanding award, as well as any awards that have been transferred without value. It is permissible to add a grant date column to the table and a related footnote detailing the vesting schedule that relates to that grant, provided the vesting schedule is the same for each covered award.

Equity Incentive Plan Awards (d), (i) and (j)

Equity incentive plan awards reported in Columns (d), (i), or (j) are based on achievement of threshold performance. However, if cumulative performance to date, as of the last completed fiscal year, exceeds threshold, then the next higher level of performance (either target or maximum) should be reported. If an award provides only for a single estimated payout, companies are to report that amount.

If an award target is not determinable, companies are to report a representative amount based on the previous fiscal year's performance.

10

OPTION EXERCISES AND STOCK VESTED

Option Exercises and Stock Vested
(for the last completed fiscal year ending xx/xx/20xx)

Name	Option Awards		Stock Awards	
	Number of Shares Acquired on Exercise (#)	Value Realized on Exercise ($)	Number of Shares Acquired on Vesting (#)	Value Realized on Vesting ($)
(a)	(b)	(c)	(d)	(e)

Disclosure must be provided on an aggregate basis for each named executive officer, and include both nonincentive (e.g., time-vesting stock options and restricted stock) and incentive (e.g., performance- vesting stock options and performance shares) plan equity awards. Equity compensation that is equitably assumed from the acquired company in an acquisition should be reported in the Options Exercised and Stock Vested Table of the acquirer company. This table (or one or more columns) may be omitted if no amounts are reportable for the last completed fiscal year covered by the table. Also, it is permissible to add one or more columns as long as it does not make disclosure misleading or unclear.

Number of Shares Acquired on Exercise (b)

The gross number of shares underlying an exercised option or SAR should be reported in Column (b), not just the net profit shares received from the exercise. Shares acquired upon option exercise that are subject to a company repurchase obligation (at the exercise price) should not be reported as option exercises in Columns (b) or (c), but rather in Columns (d) and (e) as vested stock when the repurchase obligation lapses.

Value Realized on Exercise and Vesting (c) and (e)

Value realized is the difference between the market value of the stock at the exercise/vesting date and the exercise or base price (if any). Value realized includes amounts received in connection with an award transfer for value, and excludes other payments or consideration received upon exercise/vesting (e.g., payment of exercise price or related taxes) that are properly reportable in the All Other Compensation Column (i) of the Summary Compensation Table. Footnote disclosure is required to quantify and describe the terms of any amounts realized that are deferred.

[11]

PENSION BENEFITS

Pension Benefits
(for the last completed fiscal year ending xx/xx/20xx)

Name	Plan Name	Number of Years of Credited Service (#)	Present Value of Accumulated Benefit ($)	Payments During Last Fiscal Year ($)
(a)	(b)	(c)	(d)	(e)

Disclosure is required for all tax-qualified and supplemental nonqualified defined benefit plans. This table does not require disclosure with respect to tax-qualified and nonqualified defined contribution plans. Benefits allocation between tax-qualified and supplemental nonqualified plans is based on IRS limitations as of the applicable financial statement measurement date. This table (or one or more columns) may be omitted if no amounts are reportable for the last completed fiscal year covered by the table. Also, it is permissible to add one or more columns as long as it does not make the disclosure misleading or unclear.

Plan Name (b)
Disclosure for each plan must be provided in a separate row.

Number of Years of Credited Service (c)
This number is computed as of the same measurement date used for financial statement purposes for the last completed fiscal year. If the number of years of service credited under a plan differs from the actual years of service worked, companies are to provide footnote disclosure quantifying the difference and any resulting change in benefits.

Present Value of Accumulated Benefit (d)
Present value is determined by applying the same measurement date and assumptions as are used for financial statement purposes for the last completed fiscal year. An exception is made for retirement age, which is assumed to be "normal retirement age" as defined in the plan. If normal retirement age is not defined, companies should use the earliest date that retirement can occur with no benefits reduction due to age. The accompanying narrative must disclose the valuation methodology and material assumptions, or make reference to the financial statements, footnotes to the financial statements or Management's Discussion and Analysis.

When a pension plan has a stated normal retirement age and an early retirement age at which benefits are paid without any reduction, the early retirement age should be used for determining pension benefits (the normal age may be included as an additional column). The actuarial present value of accumulated pension benefits that vest upon reaching a certain age should assume that the normal retirement age (or early retirement age, if applicable) is attained. Any actuarial "preretirement decrement" should be ignored. The present value of accumulated benefits for a cash balance pension plan is the actuarial present value of the accumulated benefits under the plan — not simply the accrued benefits.

Payments During Last Fiscal Year (e)

This column represents the dollar value of any payments and benefits paid to the named executive officers during the last completed fiscal year.

Narrative Disclosure

The material factors that are necessary to understand the amounts disclosed in the Pension Benefits Table are required in an accompanying narrative disclosure. These factors include material terms and conditions of payments and benefits available under the plan, early retirement provisions (if any), specific elements of compensation covered by the pension formula (e.g., salary, bonus), the different purposes for each plan, and any policies for granting extra years of credited service.

NONQUALIFIED DEFERRED COMPENSATION

Nonqualified Deferred Compensation
(for the last completed fiscal year ending xx/xx/20xx)

Name	Executive Contributions in Last Fiscal Year ($)	Registrant Contributions in Last Fiscal Year ($)	Aggregate Earnings in Last Fiscal Year ($)	Aggregate Withdrawals/ Distributions in Last Fiscal Year ($)	Aggregate Balance at Last Fiscal Year-End ($)
(a)	(b)	(c)	(d)	(e)	(f)

Disclosure is required on a plan-by-plan basis for all nonqualified deferred compensation and defined contribution plans, including volitional and mandatory deferrals of vested equity awards. This table does not require disclosure with respect to tax-qualified defined contribution plans, or tax-qualified and nonqualified defined benefit plans. This table (or one or more columns) may be omitted if no amounts are reportable for the last completed fiscal year covered by the table. Also, it is permissible to add one or more columns as long as it does not make the disclosure misleading or unclear.

Registrant Contributions in Last Fiscal Year (c)

Companies should include all company contributions earned during the last completed fiscal year, even if actually credited to the executive's account the following year.

Aggregate Earnings in Last Fiscal Year (d)

Companies must report all earnings on nonqualified deferred compensation, not just above-market or preferential amounts that are required to be reported in Column (h) of the Summary Compensation Table. Where plan earnings are calculated by reference to actual earnings of mutual funds or other securities (such as company stock), it is sufficient to identify the referenced security and quantify its return. Earnings include dividends, stock price appreciation or depreciation, and other similar items. Earnings also should encompass any increase or decrease in the account balance during the last completed fiscal year that is not attributable to contributions, withdrawals or distributions during the year.

Executive and Registrant Contributions (b) and (c), and Aggregate Earnings, Withdrawals/Distributions and Balance at Last Fiscal Year-End (d)-(f)

Footnote disclosure is required quantifying the extent to which amounts reported in Columns (b), (c) and (d) are reported as compensation in the Summary Compensation Table for the last completed fiscal year, and the extent to which amounts reported in Column (f) were actually reported as compensation in the Summary Compensation Table for previous fiscal years.

Narrative Disclosure

The material factors that are necessary to understand the amounts disclosed in the Nonqualified Deferred Compensation Table are required in an accompanying narrative disclosure, including:

▌ The types of compensation that may be deferred, as well as any limitations on the extent to which deferral is allowed

▌ Measures for calculating interest or other plan earnings, including whether measures are selected by the participant or company, and how often the selection may be changed

▌ Interest rates or earnings measures used during the last completed fiscal year

▌ The material terms with respect to payments, withdrawals and other distributions.

13

POTENTIAL PAYMENTS UPON TERMINATION OR CHANGE IN CONTROL

Companies are required to identify and quantify all potential compensation payments at, following or in connection with any employment termination. These termination scenarios include voluntary resignation, actual or constructive termination without cause, normal or early retirement, or change in control. The $100,000 payment threshold that existed under prior disclosure rules is eliminated.

The rules require the following:

▌ Explanation of specific circumstances that would trigger payments

▌ Description and quantification of estimated payments and benefits upon each potential triggering event, indicating whether they are payable in lump sum or installments. If a triggering event has actually occurred, disclosure is only required for that specific triggering event, even if such event occurs after the end of the last completed fiscal year, but before the proxy statement is filed

▌ Description and explanation of how various payment triggers determine payment levels

▌ Description and explanation of any restrictive covenants applicable to the receipt of payments, including noncompete, non-solicitation, non-disparagement or confidentiality agreements

▌ Description of any other material factors.

For purposes of quantifying payments, the triggering event is assumed to take place on the last business day of the last completed fiscal year based on the closing market stock price at that date. For purposes of quantifying any excise tax gross-up payments, companies may not substitute the first day of the following fiscal year for the last business day of the last completed fiscal year. Reasonable estimates (or a reasonable estimated range of amounts) are required in the event uncertainties exist.

Perquisites should be included in the quantification of payments if $10,000 or more in the aggregate, and health-care benefits should be valued using the same assumptions as used for financial statement purposes. Disclosure is not required with respect to contracts, agreements or arrangements to the extent they do not discriminate in scope, terms or operation, and are available to all salaried employees.

Pension benefits and nonqualified deferred compensation may be incorporated by reference to the respective disclosures elsewhere in the proxy statement, unless the benefits or payments are enhanced or accelerated in connection with any triggering event. Where the vesting of outstanding equity awards is accelerated, companies are to report the spread between the exercise or base price (if any) and the closing market price as of fiscal year-end to calculate the value of the awards (even if the acceleration is pursuant to a broad-based equity compensation program). Tabular presentation is encouraged under plain-English principles if it enhances disclosure.

[14]

DIRECTOR COMPENSATION

Director Compensation
(for the last completed fiscal year ending xx/xx/20xx)

Name	Fees Earned or Paid in Cash ($)	Stock Awards ($)	Option Awards ($)
(a)	(b)	(c)	(d)

Director compensation disclosure is required for anyone who served as a director during the last completed fiscal year, including those no longer serving as director at fiscal year-end or not standing for re-election the following fiscal year.

If the director also is a named executive officer, report all director compensation amounts in the Summary Compensation Table (rather than in this table), with footnote disclosures indicating which amounts are attributable to services as a director.

If the director also is a named executive officer, report all director compensation amounts in the Summary Compensation Table (rather than in this table), with footnote disclosures indicating which amounts are attributable to services as a director.

If the director is an executive officer but not a named executive officer and receives no additional compensation for services as a director, then director or executive compensation disclosure is not required, but footnote disclosure of that fact is required. One or more columns may be omitted if no amounts are reportable for the last completed fiscal year covered by the table. Also, it is permissible to add one or more columns as long as it does not make the disclosure misleading or unclear.

Fees Earned or Paid in Cash (b)

Column (b) represents all cash fees earned or paid during the last completed fiscal year, including annual retainer fees, committee and/or chairmanship fees and meeting fees. By analogy to the Summary Compensation Table for executives, this column should include any amount of cash fees converted to some other form of noncash compensation at the election of a director, with footnote disclosure describing such noncash compensation.

Stock Awards (c) and Option Awards (d)

These columns represent the same disclosures required for Columns (e) and (f) of the Summary Compensation Table for executives for the last completed fiscal

Nonequity Incentive Plan Compensation ($)	Change in Pension Value and Nonqualified Deferred Compensation Earnings ($)	All Other Compensation ($)	Total ($)
(e)	(f)	(g)	(h)

year. Companies are to provide footnote disclosure for each director of the grant date fair value of each equity award granted during the last completed fiscal year (computed in accordance with FASB ASC Topic 718), including the incremental fair value of repriced or materially modified option awards, as well as the aggregate number of nonvested stock and unexercised option awards outstanding at fiscal year-end.

Nonequity Incentive Plan Compensation (e), Change in Pension Value and Nonqualified Deferred Compensation Earnings (f) and All Other Compensation (g)

These columns represent the same disclosures required for Columns (g) through (i) of the Summary Compensation Table for executives for the last completed fiscal year. In Column (g), companies are to include consulting fees paid by the company (including fees paid by subsidiaries and/or joint ventures), and legacy and similar charitable award program benefits. Charitable matching gift programs must be disclosed, even if they do not discriminate in favor of officers or directors.

Total (h)

All amounts in this table must be reported as a single numerical value in U.S. dollars, with footnote disclosure of any necessary exchange rate conversions. This table must include all amounts earned, regardless of whether paid currently or deferred. Two or more directors may be grouped in a single row if all elements of compensation for each director are identical.

Narrative Disclosure

The material factors that are necessary to understand the amounts disclosed in the Director Compensation Table are required in an accompanying narrative disclosure, including a description of fees for retainer, committee service, service as chairman of the board or a committee, meeting attendance and any different compensation arrangements for a particular director. Tabular presentation is encouraged under plain-English principles, if it enhances disclosure.

COMPENSATION POLICIES AND PRACTICES AS THEY RELATE TO RISK MANAGEMENT

Companies are required to discuss risk considerations that have a material effect on compensation policies or decisions for named executive officers in the CD&A. In a separate section of the proxy statement, companies are required to provide narrative disclosure of their compensation policies and practices for all employees, including nonexecutive officers, if the risks associated with these programs are "reasonably likely" to have a "material adverse" effect on the company. The reasonably likely disclosure threshold is consistent with current Management Discussion and Analysis rules that require risk-oriented disclosure of known trends and uncertainties that are material to the business. The material adverse disclosure threshold is intended to help avoid voluminous and unnecessary boilerplate discussion of compensation arrangements that may mitigate inappropriate risk-taking incentives. The rules instruct companies to focus on compensation arrangements that are likely to promote risk-taking behavior that could have a significant and damaging effect on the company's operations.

A nonexclusive list of situations in which compensation programs may have the potential to raise material risks to the company and thus trigger disclosure include the following:

| A businessunit that carries a significant portion of the company's risk profile

| A business unit with compensation structured significantly differently than other units within the company

| A business unit that is significantly more profitable than others within the company

| A business unit where the compensation expense is a significant percentage of the unit's revenues

| A program that varies significantly from the overall risk and reward structure of the company, such as when bonuses are awarded upon accomplishment of

a task, while the income and risk to the company from the task extend over a significantly longer period of time.

If a company determines that disclosure is required, examples of issues that may need to be addressed include the following:

❙ The general design philosophy and implementation of compensation programs for employees whose behavior would be most affected by risk taking incentives

❙ The company's risk assessment or incentive considerations in structuring compensation programs

❙ How compensation programs relate to the realization of risks resulting from employee actions in both the near term and long term, such as clawback or equity holding period policies

❙ The company's policies regarding adjustments to its compensation programs to address changes in its risk profile

❙ Material adjustments made to compensation programs as a result of changes in the company's risk profile

❙ Extent to which compensation programs are monitored to determine whether risk management objectives are being met.

If a company determines that no disclosure is required because there are no material adverse risks, an affirmative statement indicating such determination is not required in the disclosure. However, the SEC has indicated that companies should provide a summary description of the risk assessment process and findings in their proxy disclosure. Similarly, the major proxy advisory firms expect a discussion of risk assessment process and findings, and the presence of any risk mitigating features, such as incentive compensation recovery policies. If a company elects or is required to provide narrative disclosure in regard to compensation policies and practices as they relate to risk management, such disclosure should be included with the company's other executive/director compensation proxy disclosures and not located or presented in a manner that obscures it.

16

GOLDEN PARACHUTE COMPENSATION

Golden Parachute Compensation

Name	Cash ($)	Equity ($)	Pension/NQCD ($)
(a)	(b)	(c)	(d)

Clear and simple disclosure is required in connection with any proxy or consent solicitation material seeking shareholder approval of an acquisition, merger, consolidation, or proposed sale or disposition of substantially all assets. Disclosure is also required in connection with tender offers (excluding third-party bidders), going-private transactions, and solicitations to approve the issuance of shares in a transaction, although such disclosures would but not be subject to the say-on parachute-pay advisory vote discussed in Chapter 3. The say-on-parachute-pay vote also does not apply to any arrangements between an acquiring company and the named executive officers of the target company, although such arrangements remain subject to the golden parachute compensation disclosures discussed below.

Companies that are foreign private issuers are not required to comply with the golden parachute compensation disclosures or the say-on-parachute-pay vote, unless the target company is a domestic issuer (even if the acquirer is a foreign private issuer).

This table shall include all written or unwritten compensation (whether present, deferred, contingent or nondiscriminatory) between the acquiring or target companies and the named executive officers of either company that is based on or relates to the transaction, excluding compensation related to bona fide post-transaction employment arrangements. For purposes of this disclosure in connection with a change in control transaction, the named executive officers are those reported in the Summary Compensation Table for the last completed fiscal year, as well as any chief executive officer and chief financial officer that served subsequent to the last completed fiscal year (but excluding other executives not employed at the end of the last completed fiscal year).

Companies are to provide a separate second tabular disclosure in instances where there is to be a say-on-parachute-pay vote on new or modified arrangements previously subject to a say-on-pay vote (in which case, only the new or modified arrangements subject to vote would be included in the second table), and arrangements between an acquiring company and the named executive officers of the soliciting target company (in which case, only the target company arrangements subject to vote would be included in the second table). It is permissible to

Perquisites/ Benefits ($)	Tax Reimbursements ($)	Other ($)	Total ($)
(e)	(f)	(g)	(h)

add additional named executive officers and/or one or more columns or rows to the golden parachute compensation table (for example, to distinguish between single- and double-trigger arrangement) so long as it does not make the disclosure misleading or unclear.

The tabular disclosures should be quantified assuming the triggering event takes place on the latest practicable date, using the transaction stock price to be received by shareholders (if such price is fixed) or the average closing stock price for the first five business days following public announcement of the transaction (if such price is not fixed). If the tabular disclosure is prepared in connection with a say-on-pay vote, amounts should be quantified assuming the triggering event takes place on the last business day of the last completed fiscal year based on the closing stock price at that date. In the event uncertainties exist, companies are required to make reasonable estimates and disclose such estimates (but disclosure of an estimated range of payments is not permitted).

Cash (b)

Companies are to include the aggregate value of any cash severance payments, including base salary, annual bonus, and pro-rata annual bonus or long-term incentive awards, with footnote disclosure quantifying each compensatory element included in the total and stating whether each element is conditioned on a single- or double-trigger arrangement (including time frame in which actual or constructive termination must occur for double-trigger arrangements).

Equity (c)

Companies are to include the aggregate value of nonvested stock or in-the money option awards for which vesting would be accelerated (excluding vested awards) and payments in cancellation of vested and nonvested stock or option awards, with footnote disclosure quantifying each compensatory element included in the total and stating whether each element is conditioned on a single- or double-trigger arrangement (including time frame in which actual or constructive termination must occur for double-trigger arrangements).

Pension/Nonqualified Deferred Compensation (NQCD) (d)

Companies are to include the aggregate value of pension and nonqualified deferred compensation benefit enhancements (excluding vested benefits), with footnote disclosure quantifying each compensatory element included in the total and stating whether each element is conditioned on a single- or double-trigger arrangement (including time frame in which actual or constructive termination must occur for double-trigger arrangements). This disclosure may not be incorporated by reference to the respective disclosures elsewhere in the proxy statement.

Perquisites/Benefits (e)

Companies are to include the aggregate value of perquisites and other personal benefits or property regardless of amount (even if less than $10,000), including nondiscriminatory health and welfare benefits valued using the same assumptions as used for financial statement purposes, with footnote disclosure quantifying each compensatory element included in the total and stating whether each element is conditioned on a single- or double-trigger arrangement (including time frame in which actual or constructive termination must occur for double-trigger arrangements).

Tax Reimbursements (f)

Companies are to include the aggregate value of any tax reimbursements, such as golden parachute excise tax gross ups, with footnote disclosure quantifying each compensatory element included in the total and stating whether each element is conditioned on a single- or double-trigger arrangement (including time frame in which actual or constructive termination must occur for double-trigger arrangements).

Other (g)

Companies are to include the aggregate value of any other compensation that is based on or relates to the transaction, with footnote disclosure quantifying each compensatory element included in the total and stating whether each element is conditioned on a single- or double-trigger arrangement (including time frame in which actual or constructive termination must occur for double-trigger arrangements).

Narrative Disclosure

Succinct narrative disclosure is required of material factors necessary to gain an understanding of each contract, agreement, or arrangement and the payments quantified in the table, including payment triggers, lump sum versus installment provisions, and any material restrictive covenants such as non-compete, non-solicitation, non-disparagement, or confidentiality agreements (including duration and waiver/breach provisions).

CEO PAY RATIO DISCLOSURE

For fiscal years beginning on or after Jan. 1, 2017, Companies are required disclose the annual total compensation for the median employee (excluding the principle executive officer) and the principle executive officer, and the ratio of the former to the latter. For purposes of computing the ratio, which may be presented as a reasonable estimate, companies are to set the value of annual total compensation for the median employee equal to a factor of one, such that the ratio is expressed as "x to 1" or "x:1" where "x" represents the principle executive officer's annual total compensation as a multiple of the median employee. Alternatively, companies may disclose the ratio narratively as the principle executive officer's annual total compensation as a multiple of the median employee, such that the ratio is expressed as "the principle executive officer's annual total compensation is x times that of the median employee." Companies should not disclose any personally identifiable information about the median employee other than their annual total compensation. If the pay ratio disclosure is not able to be calculated because the salary and/or bonus columns of the Summary Compensation Table are not complete at the date of proxy issuance, the company should disclose that fact and the date it expects such information to be available, at which time the pay ratio would then be disclosed on Form 8-K. Newly public companies, smaller reporting companies, and emerging growth companies must comply with the pay ratio disclosure rules for the first fiscal year commencing on or after becoming subject to SEC reporting requirements or losing status as a smaller reporting or emerging growth company, respectively. Companies are permitted to present supplemental disclosures, provided such information is clearly identified, not misleading, and not presented with greater prominence than the required pay ratio.

Annual Total Compensation

Annual total compensation is defined in accordance with the rules for calculating total compensation as reported in the Summary Compensation Table for the last completed fiscal year. Companies are permitted to use reasonable estimates when calculating annual total compensation for the median employee, with appropriate disclosure of those estimates. For non-salaried workers, references to base salary may be deemed to refer to wages and overtime. Companies are permitted to include in the calculation of annual total compensation for both the median employee and the principal executive officer special benefits and perquisites that aggregate less than $10,000 and compensation under non-discriminatory benefit plans, notwithstanding the fact that these amounts are not required to be reported in the Summary Compensation Table. In such cases, companies should disclose the differences between annual total compensation used for the pay ratio disclosure and total compensation in the Summary Compensation Table. For years in which there is more than one principle executive officer, companies must either aggregate the annual total compensation for all persons serving in that capacity during the last competed fiscal year or annualize the annual total compensation for the incumbent serving on the date the median employee is identified, with appropriate disclosure of which methodology is used.

Median Employee

The median employee is identified from the company's consolidated employee population as of a date chosen and disclosed by the company that is within the last quarter of the last completed fiscal year. Companies are permitted to identify the median employee only once every 3 years, provided there has been no change in its employee population or employee compensation arrangements that could significantly change the pay ratio disclosure. If there is a change in circumstances affecting the compensation of the median employee (for example, a significant promotion or termination of employment), companies are permitted to substitute another employee whose compensation is substantially similar to the original median employee. If the company uses the same median employee from the prior fiscal year, the company should disclose that fact and the reason(s) supporting the decision. If a company changes the date for identifying the median employee from the prior identification date, the company should disclose that fact and the reason(s) for the change.

Companies are permitted to use reasonable estimates when identifying the median employee, with appropriate disclosure of those estimates. Such reasonable estimates include the use of statistical sampling and any measure of annual total compensation that is consistently applied and reasonably reflects the annual total compensation of employees, such as cash compensation in certain circumstances or tax/payroll records, but not hourly or annual rates of pay without taking into account the number of hours actually worked. Companies may use existing internal records that reasonably reflect annual total compensation even if those records do not include every element of compensation, such as widely distributed employee equity awards. Companies are not required to use a pay period that includes the date on which the employee population is determined, nor are they required to use a full annual pay period. Companies are permitted to use a consistently applied compensation measure from the prior fiscal year provided there has not been a material change in employee population or compensation arrangements. Companies should briefly describe the methodology used to identify the median employee without resorting to technical analysis or formulas. Where a consistently applied compensation measure other than annual total compensation is used to identify the median employee, companies must disclose the compensation measure used. In such cases, it is not expected that the consistently applied compensation measure would necessarily identify the same median employee as if annual total compensation were used.

When identifying the median employee, companies are permitted to make cost-of-living adjustments to the compensation of employees in jurisdictions other than the jurisdiction of the principle executive officer. If a company elects to make cost-of-living adjustments and the median employee is identified in in a jurisdiction other than the jurisdiction of the principle executive officer, the company must use the same cost-of-living adjustment in calculating the median employee's annual total compensation. The company must disclose the jurisdiction of the median employee and the cost-of-living adjustments used to both identify the median employee and calculate annual total compensation of the median employee. In addition, the company must also identify the median employee and calculate and disclose the pay ratio without the cost-of-living adjustment. Appropriate disclosure is also required in years in which cost-of-living adjustments are adopted or discontinued..

Definition of Employee

Employee is defined as any full-time, part-time, seasonal, or temporary employee of the company or its consolidated subsidiaries. The term employee does not include leased workers or independent contractors whose compensation is determined by an unaffiliated third party. Companies may apply a widely recognized test under another area of law when determining who is an employee, such as tax or employment laws. Companies are permitted to annualize compensation for permanent full-time or part-time employees who were employed for less than the full fiscal year, such as newly hired employees or employees on leave of absence. Companies are not permitted to annualize compensation for temporary or seasonal employees, or make a full-time equivalent adjustment for any employee. Companies must determine whether furloughed workers should be included as employees based on the facts and circumstances. Companies are permitted to exclude employees from a merged or acquired company in the fiscal year in which the transaction is consummated, with appropriate disclosure of the acquired business and the approximate number of employees excluded.

Companies are permitted to exclude non-U.S. employees in foreign jurisdictions with data privacy laws or regulations that preclude compliance with the pay ratio disclosure rules. Companies taking advantage of this "data privacy exemption" must first make reasonable efforts at seeking an exemption or other relief from the data privacy laws or regulations before the non-U.S. employees may be excluded, and must disclose those laws or regulations and the company's reasonable efforts to comply. In addition, companies must obtain a legal opinion affirming the appropriateness of utilizing the data privacy exemption that must be attached as an exhibit to the filing in which the pay ratio disclosure is included. Companies are also permitted to exclude pursuant to a "de minimis exemption" up to 5 percent of their non-U.S. employees, including the non-U.S. employees excluded under the data privacy exemption. Companies taking advantage of the de minimis exemption must disclose their total number of U.S. and non-U.S. employees and the number actually used in the de minimis calculations. If a company excludes any non-U.S. employees in a particular jurisdiction under either the data privacy or de minimis exemptions, it must exclude all non-U.S. employees in that jurisdiction and disclose the name of the jurisdiction and approximate number of excluded non-U.S. employees.

18

PAY VERSUS PERFORMANCE DISCLOSURE (PROPOSED)

Pay Versus Performance
(for the last five completed fiscal year ending xx/xx/20xx)

Year	Summary Compensation Table Total for PEO ($)	Compensation Actually Paid to PEO ($)	Average Summary Compensation Table Total for non-PEO Named Executive Officers ($)
(a)	(b)	(c)	(d)

As proposed, companies would be required to add to their executive compensation disclosures tabular and narrative disclosure comparing total compensation as reported in the Summary Compensation Table to "compensation actually paid" for the principal executive officer and average other named executive officers, and cumulative total shareholder return for the company as well as a peer group for the last five completed fiscal years. Companies would be required to provide a clear description, either narratively, graphically, or both, of the relationship between compensation actually paid and the company's cumulative total shareholder return, as well as a comparison of the company's cumulative total shareholder return to that of the peer group. Companies would be required to electronically format this disclosure using eXtensible Business Reporting Language (XBRL). Companies would be permitted to submit supplemental disclosures, such as additional performance measures, graphics, and text, provided it is not misleading and not presented more prominently than the required disclosures.

Year (a)
Information is required for each of the last five completed fiscal years (three years for smaller reporting companies), or shorter period if the company is not an SEC registrant for all five years. The rules permit a phase-in during the first two years of reporting (first year for smaller reporting companies), such that only three fiscal years of information are required in the first year (two years for smaller reporting companies) and only four fiscal years of information are required in the second year.

Summary Compensation Table Total for PEO (b)
Report the amount disclosed in column (j) of the Summary Compensation Table. If more than one person served as principal executive officer for any fiscal year reported in the table, compensation amounts should be aggregated for all persons serving in that capacity for that applicable year.

Average Compensation Actually Paid to non-PEO Named Executive Officers ($)	Total Shareholder Return ($)	Peer Group Total Shareholder Return ($)
(e)	(f)	(g)

Compensation Actually Paid to PEO (c)

Calculated by taking amount disclosed in column (b) of this Pay Versus Performance Table and making the following adjustments:

Deduct	Add
The accumulated under all defined benefit and actuarial pension plans as reported in column (h) of the Summary Compensation Table (not applicable to smaller reporting companies)	The "service cost" attributable to services rendered during the last completed fiscal year under all defined benefit and actuarial pension plans. Service cost is defined by reference to the retirement benefit provisions of FASB ASC Topic 715 and includes increases value attributable to additional years of service and compensation, but excludes changes attributable to interest rates, age, and other actuarial inputs and assumptions (not applicable to smaller reporting companies)
The grant date fair value of stock and option awards reported in columns (e) and (f) of the Summary Compensation Table, respectively	The vesting date fair value of stock and option awards that vested during the year, as well as any incremental fair value attributable to previously vested awards that are repriced or materially modified during the last completed fiscal year

Companies are to provide footnote disclosure itemizing each amount that is deducted or added when calculating compensation actually paid. Footnote disclosure is also required for any assumption made in calculating the vesting date fair value of stock and option awards that differs materially from the assumptions used to calculate grant date fair value.

If more than one person served as principal executive officer for any fiscal year reported in the table, compensation amounts should be aggregated for all persons serving in that capacity for that applicable year.

Average Summary Compensation Table Total for non-PEO Executive Officers (d)

Report the average of the amounts disclosed in column (j) of the Summary Compensation Table.

Average Compensation Actually Paid to non-PEO Executive Officers (e)

The same provisions applicable to the principal executive officer in column (c) of this Pay Versus Performance Table apply to the average non-PEO officers in this column with the required footnote disclosure of amounts deducted or added expressed as averages.

Total Shareholder Return (f)

Cumulative total shareholder return is calculated using the same methodology as the stock performance graph that is required to be disclosed in Form 10-K. The measurement period begins with the closing market price on the last trading day preceding the earliest fiscal year presented in the table. This market price must be converted into a fixed investment stated in dollars. The measurement period ends with the closing market price on the last trading day of the last completed fiscal year presented in the table. For each fiscal year presented in the table, the amount reported is the cumulative total shareholder return as of the end of that year.

Peer Group Total Shareholder Return (g)

Companies are permitted to use either the same peer group presented in the stock performance graph or the peer group that is discussed in the CD&A. Companies are to identify the companies comprising the group if not a published industry or line-of-business index. Cumulative total shareholder return for the peer group is calculated in the same manner as prescribed for the company in column (f) of this Pay Versus Performance Table, except the returns for each of the companies must be weighted by market capitalization at the beginning of each fiscal year presented in the table. Smaller reporting companies do not have to comply with column (g) of this Pay Versus Performance Table.

[19   ]

INCENTIVE COMPENSATION RECOVERY POLICY AND DISCLOSURE (PROPOSED)

As proposed, companies that are listed on a national securities exchange would be required to adopt and comply with a written policy providing for the recovery of erroneously awarded (excess) incentive compensation to executive officers due to an accounting restatement due to material noncompliance with financial reporting requirements under securities laws. Companies would also be subject to new reporting requirements in their executive compensation disclosures and Form 10-K exhibits if during the last completed fiscal year an excess incentive compensation recovery process was completed or remained outstanding, the company determined not to pursue an excess incentive compensation recovery, or there was an outstanding balance of excess incentive compensation for six months or more. Companies would be required to electronically format this disclosure using eXtensible Business Reporting Language (XBRL).

Recovery Policy Requirements

The recovery policy would apply to any person who served as a Section 16 officer at any time during the performance period over which the incentive compensation is earned (regardless of when paid), and cover any incentive compensation received during the three completed fiscal years immediately preceding the date the company is "required" to prepare a restatement, regardless of when the restated financial statements are actually filed. A restatement would be considered required on the earlier of the date the company concludes (or reasonably should have concluded) the financial statements contain a material error or the date a court or regulator instructs the company issue a restatement. A restatement does not include a retrospective application of a change in accounting principles, retrospective reclassification due to a discontinued operation, or a retrospective revision to reportable segment information due to a change in the structure of a registrant's internal organization.

Incentive compensation would be defined as any compensation that is granted, earned, or vested based wholly or in part upon the attainment of a financial reporting measure, stock price, or total shareholder return. Incentive compensation would not include awards that vest solely upon the passage of time, or awards that are based on discretionary assessment or subjective goals unrelated to financial reporting measures.

Excess incentive compensation would be defined as the amount received that exceeds the amount that otherwise would have be received had it been determined based on the restated final statements, without regard for any taxes paid. In determining the amount of excess incentive compensation based on stock price or total shareholder return, companies would be required to make a reasonable estimate of the excess and provide documentation of that estimate with the applicable securities exchange.

Companies would be required to make all reasonable attempts to recover the excess incentive compensation and provide documentation of those efforts to the applicable securities exchange. Recovery would be mandatory unless it would be impracticable to do so because either the amount paid to a third party to assist in enforcing the policy would exceed the amount to be recovered, or the recovery would in the opinion of home country counsel violate home country laws established before the proposed incentive compensation recovery rules were published. Companies would be prohibited from indemnifying any current or former executive officer against the loss of erroneously awarded incentive compensation.

Recovery Policy Disclosures

If at any time during the last completed fiscal year an excess incentive compensation recovery process was completed or remained outstanding, companies are to provide the following for each restatement:

▮ Date the company was required to prepare an accounting restatement

▮ Aggregate dollar amount of excess incentive compensation attributable to such restatement

▮ Estimates that were used in determining the excess incentive compensation in event of stock price or total shareholder return measures

▮ Aggregate amount of excess incentive compensation that remains outstanding

If during the last completed fiscal year the company decided not to pursue a recovery, companies are to disclose the name and forgone amount for each affected individual as well as a brief description of the reason(s) for not pursuing recovery. If excess incentive compensation has been outstanding for six months or more, companies are to disclose the name and outstanding balance yet to be recovered for each affected individual.

Companies are to attach as an exhibit to Form 10-K the written incentive compensation recovery policy document as well as the above disclosures in XBRL electronic format.

20

OTHER RELATED DISCLOSURES

Security Ownership of Management

Companies are required to provide plain-English tabular presentation of the number and percentage of shares of each class of company stock beneficially owned by each named executive officer and director, and by all executive officers and directors as a group. For purposes of this disclosure, beneficial ownership is defined as shares of company stock over which the executive or director has sole or shared voting power, and/or sole or shared investment/disposition power (as opposed to economic or pecuniary interest).

Beneficial ownership also includes company shares that may be acquired within 60 days of the record date through the exercise of stock options or the conversion of stock units into actual stock. Thus, shares considered beneficially owned include:

❙ Shares owned outright

❙ Restricted stock

❙ Shares covered by vested and payable stock options/SARs or stock units

❙ Shares covered by stock options/SARs or stock units that will vest and become payable within 60 days of record date.

Shares not beneficially owned include cash-settled SARs or stock units, and stock-settled stock options/SARs or stock units that will not vest and become payable within 60 days of the record date. The rules require additional disclosure of the number of shares that are beneficially owned that have been pledged as security, including a "negative pledge."

Transactions with Related Persons

The rules require principles-based plain-English disclosure of any transaction or proposed transaction since the beginning of the last completed fiscal year in excess of $120,000 in which the company is a participant, and in which a "related person" has a direct or indirect material interest. Generally, related persons are defined as executive officers, directors, greater-than-5-percent shareholders or any immediate family members of each of the above persons. Also, the rules require companies to disclose their policies for review and approval of related-person transactions.

Disclosure of compensation paid to a named executive officer or director is not reportable as a related-person transaction, provided such compensation is properly reported in the executive or director compensation sections of the proxy statement, as appropriate. Disclosure of compensation paid to an executive officer who is not a named executive officer is not reportable as a related-person transaction, provided such compensation is approved by the compensation committee or board of directors.

Equity Compensation Plan Information

The SEC requires companies to include tabular information as of the end of the most recently completed fiscal year about two categories of equity compensation plans in their annual reports: equity compensation plans that have been approved by shareholders, and those that have not. In addition, companies must include this information in their proxy statements in years when submitting a compensation plan for shareholder approval.

With respect to each category, companies must disclose the:

▌ Number of shares to be issued upon option exercise or share issuance for all outstanding awards under all plans

▌ Weighted average exercise price of outstanding stock options

▌ Number of shares available for future issuance under all equity compensation plans in effect as of the end of the last completed fiscal year.

To the extent that the number of shares remaining available for future issuance includes shares that may be granted in a form other than stock options (such as restricted stock), companies should disclose the number of shares and type of plan separately for each such plan in a footnote to the table. If an equity compensation plan contains a formula for calculating the number of securities available for issuance under the plan, such as an "evergreen" formula that automatically increases the number of securities available for issuance by a percentage of the number of outstanding securities of the company, a description of this formula should be disclosed in a footnote to the table.

For purposes of this table, restricted stock grants subject to risk of forfeiture should not be reported as "Outstanding" in Column (a) or "Available" in Column (c). Conversely, stock-settled performance share units and nonqualified deferred compensation stock units should be reported as "Outstanding" in Column (a) with no "Weighted Average Exercise Price" in Column (b) and appropriate footnote disclosure acknowledging the exclusion. Shares subject to purchase under employee stock purchase plans (ESPPs) should be reported as "Available" in Column (c), not as "Outstanding" in Column (a). Companies are further required to identify and briefly describe the material features of each equity compensation plan in effect, but not approved by shareholders, as of the end of the last completed fiscal year.

Form 8-K Disclosures

The rules revise the reporting requirements of Form 8-K to generally require companies to provide a brief description of the material terms of compensatory arrangements entered into or materially modified in connection with the following triggering events:

▌ Departure of certain officers, named executive officers and directors

▌ Appointment of certain officers and election of directors

▌ Adoption or material modification of material compensatory arrangements for named executive officers (but not directors)

▌ Payment of salary or bonus previously omitted from the Summary Compensation Table for named executive officers.

"Certain officers" are defined as the PEO, president, PFO, principal accounting officer, principal operating officer or anyone performing similar functions. Form 8-K filing is required within four business days of the triggering event.

Form 10-Q and 10-K Exhibits

The following executive and director compensation arrangements are required to be filed as exhibits to Forms 10-Q or 10-K:

▌ Any compensatory plan, contract or arrangement in which any director or named executive officer participates, regardless of materiality

▌ Any other compensatory plan, contract or arrangement in which any other executive officer participates, unless immaterial in amount or significance

▌ Any equity compensation plan adopted without shareholder approval in which any employee participates, regardless of being an executive officer, unless immaterial in amount or significance.

Companies must provide an exhibit index identifying all existing plans, arrangements and contracts, as well as cite the prior or current SEC filing in which the specific document was submitted as an exhibit.

Shareholder Approval of New or Amended Plans

Finally, there is additional proxy statement disclosure when a company is soliciting shareholder approval to adopt a new cash or noncash compensation or benefits plan, or to make amendments to an existing plan. Companies are to provide a summary of the material terms of the plan or plan amendments, including the number and class of employees eligible to participate, the price of the Company's stock as of the latest practicable date, and the federal income tax consequences of the awards. Tabular disclosure of future benefits or amounts that will be received (or that would have been received had the plan or plan amendment been in place during the last completed fiscal year) by executives, directors, and other employees under the plan or amended plan is also required if such benefits or amounts are determinable.

ABOUT THE AUTHOR

Thomas M. Haines is a shareholder and Managing Director in the Chicago office of Frederic W. Cook & Co., where he has more than 28 years of board-level consulting experience in the design and implementation of executive and outside director compensation programs. Haines's consulting experience extends over a broad range of company sizes and industries, and includes projects such as total compensation reviews, annual and long-term incentive plan designs, special retention arrangements, new hire and retirement/resignation packages, and equity conversions and change-in-control provisions in connection with business acquisitions and divestitures.

Haines is a technical expert in the areas of federal tax and securities laws and U.S. accounting standards as they pertain to executive compensation, and is a frequent speaker and writer on these topics. He co-authored a book for the National Center for Employee Ownership (NCEO) titled Accounting for Equity Compensation that was a required text for the Certified Equity Professional (CEP) program. Haines is a member of the teaching faculty at WorldatWork, where he teaches advanced courses on executive compensation to industry professionals, and authors their publication on SEC executive company proxy disclosure rules now in its sixth edition. He also oversees the firm's proprietary survey database of large-company long-term incentive award levels and design provisions.

Previously, Haines was a Manager in the Minneapolis office tax practice of Ernst & Young, where he worked for 5 years. He is a Certified Public Accountant (CPA) with a master's degree in business taxation (MBT) from the University of Minnesota, a bachelor's degree in business accounting from the University of St. Thomas, and a Certified Executive Compensation Professional (CECP) designation from WorldatWork.

CPSIA information can be obtained
at www.ICGtesting.com
Printed in the USA
JSHW051505040621
15514JS00007B/6

9 781579 633939